Sustainable and environmental quality standards for hotels and restaurants

Part three: Quality management for the food and beverage division

Frank Höchsmann

Sustainable and environmental
quality standards for hotels
and restaurants

Part three:
Quality management for the food
and beverage division

Bibliographic information of the German National Library:

The German National Library lists this publication in the German National Bibliography, detailed bibliographic data is available on the internet at http: //dnb.dnb.de.

© 2022 Frank Höchsmann

Production and publishing:

BoD - Books on Demand, Norderstedt

ISBN: 9783756235650

Revision: Martha Cecilia Höchsmann Lozano / Dr. Elisabeth Strecker

Photo: St. Gilgen in Austria, stock photo

Cat's head drawing: Berlin Plaza Hotel
Authors photo: Frank Christian Höchsmann

Foreword

The hotel and tourism industry is changing worldwide and is experiencing stormy times right now. On the one hand, we are dealing with the coronavirus pandemic, on the other hand with the wave of digitalization and changes in tourists' and guests' wishes.

We have taken on these major challenges and present you with sustainable and environmentally friendly quality standards for hotels and restaurants. We have divided the quality standards into three reference books to make them handier.

The first part contains quality standards for the management, the second part contains quality standards for the hotel area and the third part contains quality standards for the restaurant area.

Our quality standards are proven in practice and approved by TÜV – Germany's number one certification organization.
This part contains the quality standards for the restaurant area: breakfast and brunch, restaurant, kitchen, and events.

By implementing sustainable and environmental quality standards, energy and water consumption is demonstrably reduced. On the other hand, the efficiency and motivation of the employees increases.

I wish you fun and success in introducing the quality standards.

With best regards, Yours

Frank Höchsmann   Berlin: July 2022

State-certified business economist in the hotel and catering industry

Graduate in Tourism Management and quality auditor
according to DIN EN ISO 9000 ff

Content

1. QUALITY STANDARDS FOR BREAKFAST AND BRUNCH......11

1.1. Work instruction: Personnel appearance 11
1.2. Work instruction: Conduct towards guests 12
1.3. Work instruction: Mise en Place 12
1.4. Workflow buffet set-up 15
1.5.Work instruction: Preparation next day 16
1.6. Workflow: service in the breakfast area 18
1.7. Work instruction: Coffee & Tea Service 21
1.8. Work instruction: Service rules 24
1.9. Checklist: Order in the breakfast room 25
1.10. Checklist for the breakfast service 26
1.11. Checklist: Reworking after 10:30 27
1.12. Circular: Appearance and team spirit 28
1.13. Job description: Breakfast manager 29
1.14. Job description: Breakfast personnel 31
1.15. Job description: Kitchen professional 33
1.16. Working Sustainably in the at breakfast 34

2. QUALITY STANDARDS FOR RESTAURANTS 35

2.1. Work instruction: Guest services 35
2.2. Work instruction: Clearing the table 37
2.3 .Work instruction: Setting the table 38
2.4. Work instruction: Taking reservations 40
2.5. Work instruction: Room Service 42
2.6. Checklist: Restaurant quality criteria 43
2.7. Checklist: Tasks Early Shift 46
2.8. Checklist: Tasks of the Service Late Shift 50

2.9. Checklist: End of Service - What to do? 52
2.10. Checklist: Cleaning in service 53
2.11. Circular: Breakage & Breakage List 55
2.12. Circular: Hygiene plan for counter 56
2.13. Circular: Restaurant service concept 57
2.14. Job description: Restaurant manager 59
2.15 Restaurant / Service Staff 61
2.16. Working sustainably at the restaurant 62

3. QUALITY STANDARDS FOR THE KITCHEN 65
3.1. Work instruction: Goods receipt CCPs 65
3.2. Work instruction: Handling fish 67
3.3. Work instruction: Handling of poultry 69
3.4.Work instructions for cooks assistants 70
3.5. Kitchen workflow 72
3.6. Food production planning: 73
3.7. Checklist: Cleaning plan / Hygiene plan 76
3.8. Checklist: Supplier evaluation 77
3.9. Checklist for activities in the kitchen 78
3.10. Circular: Temperature controls 79
3.11. Circular: Food retain samples 80
3.12. Circular: Temperature sampling 81
3.13. Job description: Chef de cuisine (Chef) 83
3.14. Job description: Sous Chef 85
3.15. Job description: Chef de Partie 87
3.16. Job description: Kitchen Professional 89
3.17. Job description: Steward 91
3.18. Form: "Break List" Kitchen 93
3.19. Working sustainably in the kitchen 94

4. QUALITY STANDARDS FOR EVENTS 97

4.1. Workflow for the events department   97
4.2. Checklist: Workflow for events   99
4.3. Checklist: Control, 48 hours before   101
4.4. Checklist: Tasks on the day of the event   102
4.5. Checklist: Service tasks event   104
4.6. Job description: Event manager   106
4.7. Job description: Assistant   108
4.8. Working sustainably in events   109

SIX STEPS TO SUCCESS 111

THE AUTHOR FRANK HÖCHSMANN 112

PUBLISHED REFERENCE BOOKS 113

SEMINARS, WEBINARS, ONLINE COURSES 114

Workshops for Professionals: 114
Workshops for Managers: 114

LAST BUT NOT LEAST, A REQUEST: 116

Notice:

- All following information is provided for information only.
- This is a presentation of the author's professional background and experience but does not claim to be exhaustive.
- No liability is assumed for the correctness of the content.
- For reasons of simplification and better readability, the masculine form is often used.
- We are committed to Article 3 of the German Constitution (Grundgesetz): equality of all people.

1. Quality standards for breakfast and brunch
1.1. Work instruction: Personnel appearance

Our appearance is very important for the first impression and the further course at breakfast and brunch: therefore, these points should be observed by every employee:

1. Clothing/dress code:
   - black trousers clean and ironed
   - Shirt clean and ironed, apron in summer, according to dress code
   - black shoes (shone) and black socks
   - department-specific uniform with name badge and bag
2. Appearance:
   - well-groomed hair (tie up long hair, no brightly coloured hair), careful (daily) shaving
   - clean and well-groomed fingernails (no coloured nail varnish)
   - no piercing or long earrings, for men no ear jewellery
   - discreet make - up
   - discreet deodorant
3. Taboos in the guest area:
   - chewing gum
   - eating and drinking (also at the bar)
   - leaning against walls, furniture etc.
   - finger your face
   - hands in the trouser pockets
   - talking about guests (gossiping)
   - lecturing guests
   - reading newspapers
   - nose blowing, snorting, nose blowing in the guest area
   - mobile phones, private telephone calls during working hours

1.2. Work instruction: Conduct towards guests

Guests judge our house by your appearance, behaviour, and demeanour. The impression you convey is a decisive factor in deciding whether a guest will return to our hotel. This includes a friendly welcome and attentive service. A smiling face is always nicer than a grim one. We are the hosts and convey to the guest that they are welcome as soon as they enter the restaurant!

The guest should feel cosseted by you and not just provided for. The guest remains YOUR guest until he or she has left the house, even after payment. The last impression is just as important as the first. That is why a friendly farewell, in which you thank them for their visit, is very important.

You are the professional and the guest expects you to perform well.

Small service - etiquette / etiquette rule

- Look for eye contact with guests!
- Nod, as a sign of recognition - when you are busy!
- Work with your head - not with your feet, no unnecessary ways!
- Do not do to others what you do not to be want done to you!
- Smile, look friendly and open!
- Look after the guest in a courteous way - not just provide for him!
- The guest is YOUR guest, be a – HOST not a dish carrier!

1.3. Work instruction: Mise en Place
Order of items

1. Provide all the necessary items for a flawless service at your workplace.
2. All non-food items are to be ordered by the head of department. Let us know in good time if something runs out
3. The table linen can be taken from the linen store at any time (please pay attention timely)

Cleanliness of all items

Attention must be paid to cleanliness and perfect condition of all service items, this includes:

- do not use chipped porcelain or glass in the guest area, dispose of these in the respective breakage bins and note it on the breakage list.
- cutlery should never be tarnished or bent.
- cutlery is polished by service and stewarding staff before use in the guest area. Use water sparingly. Use vinegar!
- salt cellar and pepper pot are filled up (at least 2/3 full) .and the holes are free
- the sugar bowls are filled up with sugar/sugar sticks and they are clean
- the spoons are clean
- milk jugs are filled with fresh milk, there are no dried rims in the jug.
- daily cleaning of the chafing dishes is compulsory and is carried out and checked by the kitchen staff
- flower vases: The flowers in the vases are fresh, look fresh. There is enough fresh water in the vases.

The table is set as follows

- Flower vase with flowers in the middle

- saltshaker and pepper pot (see photo)
- The sugar bowl should never stand on the fold of the tablecloth,
- the below fold of the tablecloth directed to the entrance; the guest looks over the below fold to the above fold
- note that the distance to the flower vase and the arrangement are the same for all tables. This provides an overall appearance
- it should also be noted that at tables for several people, the number of cruets stands, and cream jugs should be increased accordingly.
- centre cutlery: centre fork on the left, centre knife on the right) in the middle of the napkin
- the cutlery is parallel / at right angles to the edges of the table and 5 mm in distance from it.
- the coffee cup stands upside down on a saucer. The upper edge of the saucer is f at with the tip of the knife. The cup is aligned for the handle and the coffee spoon to point to the edge of the table at a 45° angle to the bottom right (04:20h).

Mise en Place in the breakfast kitchen

- the mise en place is prepared by a breakfast staff member according to the number of guests.

1.4. Workflow buffet set-up

All employees must be dressed and at workplace 10 minutes before the start of work!

1. switch on the coffee machine
2. switch on the chafing dishes
3. switch on grill and oven
   and bake buns

> 160 degrees, 15minutes
>
> Set convectomat to „combi" (humidity and heat)

4. put cooling packs under the breakfast plates
5. switch on samovar, full power
6. put bacon on to fry
7. put eggs on to boil, boil for 5 minutes!
   Soft eggs at guest's request only with signature (archive form for 2 weeks, risk of salmonella).
8. check eggs and bacon at regular intervals. Finally, scramble the eggs and place in the chafing dish.
9. Prepare sausage and cheese platters, tomatoes, cucumbers, yoghurt, milk and juices (service), jams and marmalades, tomato juice, honey and Nutella, fruit platters, butter, margarine etc.
10. set up the buffet according to the plan (see photos)
11. set up muesli buffet the evening before, check in the morning
12. set up rolls and bread corner, also rusks and crispbread.
13. service staff: Brew coffee and fill it into thermos flasks.
14. service staff: Put coffee pot and creamer on the tables
15. Service staff: Place cutlery on the tables and regularly check for cleanliness or replace it.
16. Important: Check the buffet at short intervals to see if anything needs to be replenished or cleaned up!!!!

1.5. Work instruction: Preparation for the next day

Sausage/cheese platters	For up to 20 persons one nicely garnished platter with sausage and one with cheese. At full capacity, place all available platters
Smoked salmon tartare	From 20 persons on, 3 small slates Form balls with the smallest ice cream scoop, garnish with horseradish and display in a separate bowl
Fruit/fruit salad	Always a nice platter of whole fruits, a bowl of fruit salad, and up to 40 persons a large round platter of sliced fruits

Fruit:

From 40 persons on a large oval platter.

From 80 persons on, one large round platter and one large oval platter.

Yoghurts:

Always mix a large bowl of fruit yoghurt / curd , no matter how high the occupancy is.

Fresh vegetables:

A platter with fresh cucumber slices and fresh tomato wedges is always placed on the buffet.

Salads:

There are always 3 different homemade salads in small glass bowls on the buffet.

Cake:

A homemade cake or muffin is always placed on the buffet in rotation.

Note:
The number of plates varies with the number of guests!

1.6. Workflow: service in the breakfast area

A) General:

The breakfast service personnel is composed as follows

1. Breakfast manager
2. Waiter, service staff / temporary staff
3. Person responsible for buffet and kitchen
4. Stewarding

B) Preparation:

- Open rooms, switch on lights, ventilate, switch on heating if necessary.
- Check tables laid
- Prepare the buffets and carry out the kitchen work (eggs, bacon, etc. by the kitchen staff). Service personnel controls buffet arrangements
- Set up juices and milk service station next to guest entrance
- Distribute the cream jugs to the tables
- Distribute thermos jugs with coffee to the service stations. Only thermos jugs that are in good condition and clean are used.
- Only the large thermos jugs are used at breakfast.
- Prepare Mise en Place
- Each employee informs himself/herself with the breakfast management
- Turn on music

C) Service:

- Welcome the guests
- Ask for beverage request. When serving coffee pour the cup for the guest
- For all other hot beverages, the service standards "Serving hot beverages" applies.
- The guest serves himself at the breakfast buffet with dishes, cold milk and juices.
- Fulfil individual wishes of the guests as far as possible. E.g., request for egg dishes up to 15 persons
- During the entire service, care must be taken to ensure that the table is tidy and clean (clearing away used crockery and glasses. The guests only must find what they need at their place at any time)!
- After the guest has left the table, it has to be re-arranged, , i.e. the crumbs are wiped off the table with a napkin onto a plate
- All service in the breakfast area is done with the trays provided for breakfast
- Thermos jugs are carried in the hand
- All work, such as clearing away, setting the table, if necessary, tea service, is carried out with clean trays with napkins and cutlery bags if necessary.

D) Clearing:

Generally, observe the following.

1. Avoid noise when clearing away
2. Cleanliness at the clearing station
3. cleanliness of the floor
4. The rubbish is sorted according to cardboard, food leftovers, packaging).

5. Handle glass and porcelain with care to avoid breakage or damage.
6. Put the jam bowl in a bucket of water like the cutlery

E) After breakfast

- Checking the tables in the restaurant, changing linen if necessary
- Arrange restaurant newly for lunch service
- Arrange the restaurant for events, if so.
- The chairs are checked for stains and cleaned if necessary. If the chairs are very dirty, please inform cleaning
- The restaurant is left in a clean and tidy condition.
- Check the amount of laundry available

1.7. Work instruction: Coffee & Tea Service (example)

Welcoming the guest

Every guest is greeted with a friendly "good morning". Every single member of staff must be aware that the impression they leave with guests will be their first and lasting impression of the service and of our restaurant. That is why friendly and attentive service, especially early in the morning, is so infinitely important!

And don't forget:
A smiling face is always prettier than a grim one!!!

Coffee and tea service as well as milk and cocoa service

1. After the guest has taken a seat and been greeted in a friendly manner, we ask if he will have coffee.
   Important: Questions are asked in complete sentences e.g.: "Good morning. May I pour you some coffee?

2. Coffee:
   If possible, the cup is lifted and the first cup is poured.

   Coffee is made in the coffee kitchen if required. We use soluble coffee powder, 2 teaspoons and fill with hot water, stir once, and serve in a porcelain pot (with lid!).

3. Tea: (bag tea)
   - Green tea
   - Black tea
   - Herbal tea
   - Peppermint tea

   If a guest requests tea, our selection of tea should be offered and reference made to the tea buffet. It goes without saying that in particularly hectic situations, it is not necessary to list the entire range of our teas; the same applies to foreign-language tour groups. When serving, indicate the time of infusdion..

Since tea is an infusion drink, the tea bag is first placed in the glass and then filled with hot water. With the black teas, the question of milk/cream or lemon should not be forgotten.

4. Hot milk & cocoa - in a porcelain pot
- Warm milk and hot chocolate are taken from the machine
- We are happy to fulfil special requests for other drinks, but these are not included in the breakfast price. Cold drinks that are not on the breakfast buffet must also be paid for by the guest.

Table control

Generally, there is only as much crockery on the table as the guest still needs.

Please pay special attention to half-empty coffee creamer jugs, large plates for egg dishes and empty cereal bowls. If you are not sure whether the used plates can be cleared yet, politely ask the guest before piles of plates start to build up. Always re-arrange the tables immediately after a guest has left the table. Wipe down the table before setting it and put on a new tablecloth and place mats. Do not forget the napkins. Then set the coffee cups and cutlery.
One piece of crockery should always remain with the guest (coffee cup or glass) to give him/her the feeling of not being thrown out.

Set the table

All tables are set in the same way. Same way means that, for example, cruets and vases are always in the same place.

Belongs on every table:

- Filled salt and pepper menages
- Coffee cream and sugar
- a flower vase

A place is set for each guest:

- 1 x paper napkin
- 1x medium cutlery
- 1 x cup, and coffee spoon (handle and spoon at 04:30)

Even if there are many breakfast guests, please make sure that the cutlery is not placed on the table to be arranged afterwards. It is also not polished with the polishing cloth at the table, in front of the guest!

1.8. Work instruction: Service rules

1. The stations are always occupied with personnel

2. Approach the guests (friendliness)

3. Work quickly, as inconspicuously and silently as possible

4. Make sure if the guests still have wishes, if so: fulfil them

5. Feel like a host who gives his guests a good start to the day

6. In case of ambiguities (linguistic or similar), always make sure to ask a second time in a friendly manner or ask for help from your superior.

7. Don't get hectic, it doesn't make the work go faster.

1.9. Checklist: Order in the breakfast room

(Please use this list daily)

OK	Activity/work instruction	Comment/ Responsibility
	Tables and chairs are neatly aranged	
	Tables are set according to the service rules	
	Buffets are clean and tidy (breakfast room)	
	Curtains/ drapes hang neatly (restaurant/ breakfast room)	
	Temperature is pleasant	
	The floor is clean	
	The ventilation grills are clean	
	Lighting is pleasant	
	Volume and music comply with the specifications (note guest groups)	
Verified:		Date/Time:

1.10. Checklist for the breakfast service

Please apply daily

1. Check the cleanliness of the breakfast room against the checklist
2. Check cleanliness of utensils using the checklist
3. Prepare the breakfast buffet according to the following principles:
   - From savoury to sweet
   - From cheap to expensive
   - Little of the perishables
   - Principle of freshness and completeness
   - Principle of perfect guest care

4. Welcome the guest
5. Welcome regular guests by name
6. Show them where to sit, maybe briefly explain the breakfast buffet or list the range of products.
7. Ask for requests (tea/coffee, eggs, special requests)
8. Pay special attention to diabetics / sick / ailing people
9. Pour first cup
10. Show the guest where to pour from (samovar and / or coffee pot)
11. Refill buffet, clear used plates
12. Prepare invoice / inform reception
13. Farewell: Express thanks and wish a good journey
14. Clear, supply, refill, reorder
15. Record special issues, inform management
16. Re-arrange the restaurant to perfection
17. Other activities not listed here

1.11. Checklist: Reworking after 10:30

Rework breakfast buffet and breakfast room, after 10.30 a.m.

1st Clear the buffet
2nd Get food for the next day
3rd Clear tables
4th Change tablecloths
5th Re-arrange for breakfast if there is no extra event in the meantime
6th Check sugar bowls for cleanliness, clean if necessary
7th Fill the sugar bowls
8th Clean the cruet stands
9th Fill up the cruets, leaving 1 cm of space to the caps .
10th Clean the buffet
11th Clean signs and prepare them for the next day
12th Fill up the muesli
13th Clean and refill juice dispenser
14th Clean the milk container, including the tap
15th Empty bread baskets (kitchen personnel)
16th Clean chafing dishes, change water (kitchen personnel)
17th Clean the samovar
18th Fill up tea
19th Fill up sweetener
20th Distribute clean dishes to the stations
21st Clean service tables
22nd Distribute cutlery / cutlery bags to the service tables
23rd   VIP - Prepare and distribute place settings or pass on to lunch service
24th Check carpet for stains
25th Dust chairs
26th Check and clean chair covers
27th Fill and folding napkins
28th Dispose off the waste

1.12. Circular: Appearance, behaviour, and team spirit

1st   A positive attitude, discipline, open-mindedness, enthusiasm and a natural sense of service are among the basic characteristics.

2nd   Punctuality and a well-groomed appearance are basic requirements for every service employee. Everyone must be punctual and well-groomed when starting work.

3rd   Jewellery, hairstyle, clothing, and make-up are to be kept discreet.

4th   A genuine smile is catching- also with our guests. It is simple, for free and signalizes the guests that they are welcome here.

5th   Team spirit, helpful and considerate co-operation are a matter of course for us.

6th   To ensure a smooth service process, please check out with your department head before going to the restroom so that he/she can ensure that your station is taken care of.

7th   A service employee anticipates guest requests. Every guest request must be taken seriously.

8th   Even under time pressure, every guest is a V.I.P. We make every guest feel welcome and never turn back anyone.

9th   Guests always have priority.

10th   During a conversation, always maintain eye contact with the respective person.

11th   Have private conversations of any kind in the break or after work.

12th   The colloquial language among the staff is English.

13th   Guests should not have the feeling that they are being talked about!!!

14th   Discussions of any kind must not be held in presence of guests or during business.

1.13. Job description: Breakfast manager

Hotel / restaurant	
Department:	Food and beverage
Position name	Breakfast manager
Position holder:	Name of the current position holder
Position holder reports to:	Restaurant manager
Co-operation with:	All colleagues
Subordinatedpersonnel :	Trainees and apprentices
The position holder can represent:	The head of food and beverage department
Deputy:	Colleagues
Aim of the position:	Excellent breakfast service leading to maximum guest satisfaction The breakfast manager is mainly responsible for the breakfast. In addition, he is responsible for the supervision of events. He co-operates closely with the restaurant manager and reports to him.
Job descriptions/ Tasks and responsibilities	<ul><li>Looking after the breakfast guests</li><li>Assistance in the banquet area and restaurant</li><li>Ordering and receiving goods</li><li>Product selection for the breakfast buffet</li><li>Quality control of the products</li><li>Briefing and instruction of employees, apprentices, and trainees</li><li>Checking the report books of the trainees</li><li>Provision of the VIP gifts</li><li>Control of the breakfast kitchen according to HACCP</li></ul>

	• Collaboration in stewarding in the breakfast kitchen • Preparing the hot and cold dishes for the breakfast buffet • Carrying out other activities not listed here but ordered by the restaurant management at short notice
Work equipment:	• Hardware and (restaurant / banquet) software • QMH with the applicable quality documents
Working conditions:	Depending on requirements, also irregular working hours, especially on Sundays and holidays
Special authorities:	May be granted domestic authority

Taken notice: Place & Date:

1.14. Job description: Breakfast personnel

Hotel / restaurant:	
Department:	Food and beverage
Position name	Breakfast service staff
Position holder:	Name of the current position holder
Jobholder reports to:	Breakfast manager / restaurant manager
Co-operation with:	All colleagues in the food and beverage department, the reception and housekeeping
Subordinate personnel:	Trainees and apprentices
The position holder can represent:	The head of F & B department / restaurant manager / breakfast manager
Deputies:	Colleagues
Aim of the position:	The breakfast service personnel work mainly in the breakfast area. In addition, they help at events when needed.
Job descriptions/ Tasks and responsibilities	<ul><li>Serving food and drinks</li><li>Looking after the breakfast guests</li><li>Assistance in the conference/banquet area / restaurant</li><li>Ordering and receiving goods</li><li>Product selection for the breakfast buffet</li><li>Quality control of the products</li><li>Instruction and briefing of trainees and interns</li><li>Looking after the VIP guests</li><li>Provision of the VIP gifts</li><li>Cleaning the breakfast kitchen according to HACCP</li><li>Collaboration in stewarding in the breakfast kitchen</li><li>Preparing the hot and cold dishes for the breakfast buffet</li><li>Carrying out other activities not listed here but ordered by the restaurant management at short notice</li></ul>

Work equipment:	• Hardware and (restaurant/banquet) software • Quality management handbook with the quality documents in force
Working conditions:	• Depending on requirements, also irregular working hours, especially on Sundays and public holidays
Special authority :	• May be granted domestic authority

Taken notice/ Signature: Place/date:

1.15. Job description: Breakfast kitchen professional

Hotel /Restaurant	Name
Department:	Kitchen
Position name:	assistant cook, breakfast kitchen professional
Position holder:	Name of the current position holder
Reports to	Chef
Co-operation with:	All F&B department
Subordinated personnel	Trainees, apprentices, temporary staff
The position holder can be represented:	Colleagues
Deputies :	Colleagues on an equal footing
Objective of theposition :	Execution of activities in connection with breakfast and preparations for the a la carte business and/or half board
Tasks and responsibilities	• Breakfast platters (cold cuts) • Fruit plate • Eggs and scrambled eggs • Breakfast meatballs / mini meatballs • Nuremberg sausages • Bacon/breakfast bacon • Egg, herring, meat, sausage salad • Baking bread and rolls
Requirements	• Supervision of trainees and apprentices
Work equipment:	• Kitchen utensils and equipment • Raw goods and semi-finished or finished products • Measuring instruments (thermometers), checklists, work instructions, plans
Working conditions:	• Depending on requirements, also irregular working hours, Sundays and public holidays
Special authorities:	• Has further powers which are specified in the employment contract,

Taken notice: Signature: Place/date:

1.16. Working Sustainably in the at breakfast

Evaluation criteria for breakfast	10/9 ☺☺	8/7 ☺	6/5 ☺	4/3 ☹	2/1 ☹☹
Green electricity from renewable sources (sun, wind, water, biomass)					
Organic eggs from the organic farm next door					
Homemade jam / marmalade					
Honey from the area, from the regional beekeeper					
Food regional, seasonal (meat, cheese, vegetables, etc.)					
Bread rolls from the local bakery					
Ecological napkins, biodegradable, unbleached					
Sort waste, organic waste on the compost heap					
Environmental training for the breakfast staff					
No plastic used					
Total points					
Suggestions:					

2. Quality standards for Restaurants
2.1. Work instruction: Guest services

- **First contact**: The guest's first contact with our house is crucial and cannot be made undone. All staff members are aware of this. However, this first contact can take place directly or indirectly. Our future guests receive their first information about our restaurant through recommendations (friends, acquaintances, family), advertising material (catalogues, flyers, advertising brochures), telephone information, websites, information at travel agencies or tourist information offices and tour operators. All staff are encouraged to make suggestions for improvement.
- **Reservation/booking**: Table reservations are often made directly (by telephone or verbally). Bookings for events are made via our reception and/or the events office. All staff in this area work according to the work instructions Proper Telephoning and Selling. Reservation forms are filled out correctly and written confirmation is offered. Reservations of tables up to a maximum of 8 persons are possible without further coordination, above this with the agreement of the restaurant management / kitchen. Record data and offer a call-back.
- **Restaurant room**: The service staff sets up the restaurant room to make daily business run smoothly. They receive instructions from the department or shift manager. Realizing and acting autonomously are very important here.
- **Mise-en-place**: Includes the preparation work of the service staff. The respective work instruction focuses on the preparations to be made for lunch or dinner business, in particular setting the tables, setting upt side tables /placing stations, decorations, replenishing the cruets. Ensure a "uniform" styling in the restaurant. The setting of the tables is done according to the standards of the house. For extraordinary occasions, the department head / shift supervisor prepares a daily plan with the corresponding specials / instructions (functions, birthday tables, etc.).
- **Service/guest care**: Our service or guest care proceeds in the following steps: first we welcome our guests, take their wardrobe,

then we seat them and ask for their wishes and/or advise them and recommend an aperitif in advance. Depending on the situation, we hand over the menu and take requests a little later (always ask about intolerances and inform the kitchen!!!). We take the drinks order immediately after the seating. We serve the food and drinks without delay and in the order: ladies before gentlemen and old before young. Exceptions are possible (birthdays, anniversaries, guests of honour, e.g., to avoid confusion at large tables (10 persons or more).:

- **The bill** is brought and discreetly handed over at the guest's request. The guest pays in cash or by credit card.
- **Food and drinks:** We make sure that the food and drinks meet our high-quality standards and are served in a timely manner. We serve drinks within 5 minutes and food within 15-25 minutes (exceptions are possible).
- In case of discrepancies (with other departments) and complaints, we turn to the senior manager deputy restaurant manager, restaurant manager.
- Aftercare: Depending on the type of action, the aftercare is controlled by the reception or the management.
- Mobile phone ban, use only allowed during breaks, exceptions only for work-related phone calls.

Taken notice: _____date: ___

2.2. Work instruction: Clearing the table

Activity	Who?
1. Every table in the restaurant is in perfect condition at any service time	
2. Dirty plates and cutlery are cleared from the right after we have made sure that the guest has finished eating .	
3. IMPORTANT! Don't forget the bread plates and the unnecessary cutlery, even for buffet guests.	
4. Glasses and other utensils (cruets, vinegar and oil, pepper mill) are also cleared (with a tray) from the right.	
5. When clearing the table, please make sure that we do not soil or stain the guest.	
6. The clearing is done quietly.	
We try to fulfil every special request of our guests and to recognize their needs, such as newspaper (especially when guests are alone), dog bowls, power sockets for mobile phones and laptops, sensitively and early and thus are good hosts!	

2.3. Work instruction: Setting the table

Standards	Who?
1. the napkin is always placed in the centre of the place setting, taking into account the different shapes.	
2. setting is done from inside to outside	
3. Cutlery, bread plate and napkin of a place setting lie at the same distance from the edge of the table (about a finger wide) Exception: the starter fork lies offset upwards so that the prongs of the starter fork begin where the prongs of the main course fork end.	
4. Viewed from above, one piece of cutlery never covers another	
5. the bread knife is placed on the right edge of the bread plate	
6. the reference glass is always in line with the main course knife, about a finger wide away.	
7. the dessert fork lies centrally at the level of the centre of the reference glass with the prongs to the right	
8. the dessert spoon lies exactly above the dessert fork with the handle to the right	
9. Cutlery pieces of two opposite place settings are on one line (main course fork on one line with the opposite main course knife, etc.)	
10. Glasses of a place setting are aligned with the candle or the centre of the table.	
11. Glasses of two place settings facing each other are also aligned	

Detailed handling and set up follow here in detail.

A la Carte • Distribute napkins • To the right of ithe napkin the large knife is placed • Putthe large fork on the left of the napkin • (please always leave a gap of 1 thumb's width, approx. 1 cm, from the lower edge of the table). • A bread plate with butter knife is placed on the same height of the fork on the left (some distance to the fork) • Candle, flowers, cruets	
HB- (half board in a hotel with restaurant) • Place 2 sets of fork and knife • Dessert cutlery above the napkin (spoon lies above the fork) • Bread plate and knife as for á la carte • Spoon is set if there is a 4-course menu or kitchen sends 3-courses with soup • Put up reserved signs (with family name) • Menu (logo points to the entrance)	
Breakfast set up • Place napkins • Left: fork, right: knife • To the right of the knife, the saucer is placed with the cup and spoon • (Handle of cup and spoon point to approx. at 4:20h) • Sugar containers are additionally placed • Put displays: with coffee specialities on the tables	
Buffet for conference guests: • Napkins (shape: classic) • Placeknife & fork	

2.4. Work instruction: Taking reservations

Taking table reservations	
Table reservations up to 15 people for food only, larger events are booked via events department.:	Take reservation book software at hand Get an overview of whether a reservation is still possible. If you do not have an immediate overview, accept the reservation but do not confirm it as binding, arrange a call-back. Note the reservation in the reservation book / software under the appropriate date and time of day (noon / evening) Note name, first name, (make visible whether lady or gentleman has reserved) Note telephone number, number of people, time, other wishes (e.g., menu or flowers). Do not make promises! Offer menu, if necessary, plan or forward the call to kitchen (Offer guest to send follow up suggestions by email - record email address)
Table reservations of over 20 people:	Forward the conversation to **events department** If no staff member is available→ Inform caller that staff member is not available now, requests will be noted, call-back will be made at the earliest possible time. Note everything as "call note" (reservations) Note name, title or first name (make visible whether the caller is a gentleman or a lady), telephone number, when the caller can be called back, reservation date, number of persons, date and time of the call, signature. Do not make promises
Conference / seminar / room / event enquiry	
Forwarding conversations	Forwarding to sales department or reception manager
No employee of sales department available	Notification that these reservations are being processed by the sales department,

	but unfortunately no person of the sales department is available at the moment. However, requests will be noted, call-back will be made at the next possible opportunity. Note everything as "call note" (reservations): Name, company if applicable, telephone number if available, reservation date, number of persons. If caller already expresses further wishes, note them down, but do not ask for them! When requesting a personal reservation on site, show guest our premises on request and note what was shown Compare the notes Ensure call-back Note in reservation book / software

2.5. Work instruction: Room Service

(This instruction is valid for restaurants at a hotel)

1. Phone calls to the restaurant are responded to immediately and the order is taken correctly
2. The employee repeats the order on the phone and books the room service fee. The employee informs the guest about the amount of the fee.
3. The room service place setting is complete and served in a presentable condition: (- In the evening work with cloche / pepper and salt in bags, cloth napkins., At breakfast pay attention to the guest's order list.
4. Room Service -orders must be delivered within half an hour
5. The trays are in a clean condition
6. On the service tray there is a card "Please call the restaurant after your meal. We will be happy to clear the arrangement.
7. Tray with napkin, fork and knife, glass or cup and saucer, pepper and salt in bags and in addition milk and sugar for breakfast.
8. The guest is presented with the bill in a leather folder and pen for signature
9. Room service is available from 7:00 a.m. to 9:00 p.m.

2.6. Checklist: Restaurant quality criteria

#	Criteria	Rating/Comment 10 = points excellent
01.	First contact	
1.	Telephone ringing (3-5 times only)	
2.	Correct/polite	
3.	Name of the guest	
4.	Restaurant information	
5.	Internet presence	
6.	Advertising material	
7.	Table reservation	
8.	Signage	
9.	Parking	
10.	Facade	
02.	Restaurant room	
11.	Entrance doors	
12.	Odours	
13.	Light	
14.	Colours	
15.	Noises/music	
16.	Temperature	
17.	Decoration	
18.	Room layout	
19.	Furnishings	
20.	Atmosphere/ambience	
21.	Other rooms	
03.	Guest seats	
22.	Table	
23.	Chair	
24.	Style	
25.	Logical arrangement	
26.	Harmony	
04.	Mise-en-place	
27.	Tablecloth	
28.	Runner	
29.	Place setting	
30.	Cutlery	
31.	Glasses	
32.	Plates	
33.	Cruets / Salt Shakers	
34.	Napkins	
35.	Side tables	
36.	Side tables	
37.	Reserve utensils/cutlery	
05.	Menuss	
38.	Menu	

39.	Wine lists/beverage lists	
40.	Dessert/Ice Cards	
41.	Attractive design	
42.	Clean	
43.	Logical order of content	
44.	Well arranged	
45.	Price information correct	
46.	Current offers	
47.	Starters cold-warm	
48.	Soups	
49.	Fish	
50.	Roast and grilled dishes	
51.	Game and poultry	
52.	Desserts	
53.	Cheese and fruit	
54.	Specialities of the house	
55.	Dishes of the day	
56.	Children's/seniors' plates	
57.	Cold dishes /Small menu	
06.	Service/guest care	
58.	Welcome	
59.	Placement	
60.	Handing over menus	
61.	Recording the drinks orders	
62.	Serving the drinks	
63.	Recording the food orders	
64.	Serving the food	
65.	Advice and assistance	
66.	Clearing tables	
67.	Invoice	
68.	Good-bye	
07.	Food/consumed food	
69.	Quality	
70.	Quantity	
71.	Appearance	
72.	Colour combination	
73.	Texture	
74.	Smell	
75.	Meat/sides/garnishing	
76.	Sauce	
77.	Plate	
08.	Drinks/consumed drinks	
78.	Quality	
79.	Quantity	
80.	Fresh	
81.	Temperature	
82.	Proper glasses	
83.	Sufficient offer	
84.	Beverage advice	

85.	House wine	
09.	Staff	
86.	Courteous	
87.	Open	
88.	Accommodating	
89.	Ready for service	
90.	Charismatic	
91.	Impeccable outfit	
92.	Correct posture	
93.	Languages	
94.	Pronunciation	
95.	Willing to learn	
10.	Price-performance ratio	
96.	adequate	
97.	Not adequate	
98.	Comparable with competition	
99.	Locally comparable	
100.	Price leadership	
	Total	

Quality assessment

☐	Outstanding: 100-91	☐	Satisfactory 70-61
☐	Very good: 90-81	☐	Poor 60-51
☐	Good: 80-71	☐	Insufficient: 50-00

Taken notice : _____ date: ___

2.7. Checklist: Tasks of the Service - Early Shift

These tasks are to be done from 6:00 to 7:00 a.m.

- o Read the shift book and observe the information board / intranet page
- o Switch on kitchen light
- o Set up coffee machine + milk frother
- o Prepare coffee
- o Switch on lights in the buffet room
- o Turn on music
- o Set up breakfast buffet
- o Set the serving cutlery
- o Prepare hot milk
- o Distribute coffee milk jugs (place next to sugar container on tables)
- o Distribute coffee pots (meetings & bus trips).
- o Private guests are asked for coffee, and it is served in small jugs
- o Final check for completeness and cleanliness
- o Switch on all lights
- o Unlock all doors
- o Switch on Glass washing machine

These tasks are to be done from 7:00 to 11:00h (e.g.)

- Checking whether there are reserved signs on the tables or whether tables must be prepared for special occasions.
- Private guests and docents: seat, check for coffee, bring coffee pot to the table, if there are no fried/scrambled eggs at the buffet, check and order in the kitchen
- Training courses and buses: Overnight guests usually have the same table as the previous evening
- New arrivals: if coffee or breakfast buffet is included in the package, inform guests of this.
- Ask guests about satisfaction & wishes (more coffee. etc.)
- Check buffet again and again, refill if necessary & keep clean
- Clear the tables and clean up with a small service broom, scraper or cloth napkin.
- Replace tablecloths
- Terrace: tablecloths and ashtrays in fine weather,
- Open sunshades
- Place candles, flowers & cruets neatly time and again
- Sweep chairs, benches (service hand broom), align chairs
- Wash glasses, polish them and bring them back to the restaurant
- Polish cutlery
- FROM 10.30 a.m. Clear the breakfast buffet:
- First put food that needs to be cooled into cold storage (jam, tomato juice, yoghurt, fruit, milk, plates).
- Bread, cake, eggs into the kitchen
- Muesli, grains, honey & Nutella are replenished and taken away into the respective cupboard underneath
- Put egg cups, glass bowls under the buffet
- Clean the buffet room
- Clean juice bar, glass bonnets, all surfaces, cheese dome, clear crumbs from bread baskets

These tasks are to be done from 11:00 to 15:00h (e.g.)

- Clear and clean coffee buffet, tea station

- Put tea stand, coffee, sweetener in the cupboard below
- Move samovar, coffee & milk to the kitchen
- Place the sugar bowls in the designated cupboard
- If there is, make preparations for lunch buffet
- 12.00 Lunch service
- Assigning works to service staff
- Clarification of seating for event participants
- Clarification if & how many drinks are free
- Beverage service
- Lunch buffet: Advertise it to guests
- Menu: Call-off in the kitchen when all participants of a group are there
- Docents: quickest possible service, usually drink cappuccino, latte etc. after the meal
- Private guests: see Instruction on private guests' service
- Buses: food mostly pre-ordered, beverage service, call-off of food in the kitchen
- In case of a menu: Clear plates when all guests at a table are finished
- For buffet: when plate is empty - clear away
- Clear empty glasses, ask for another drink
- Clean tables, change tablecloths, if necessary, re-arrange chairs
- Re-arrange candles, flowers, cruets
- When all guests have left, clear buffet area, the lunch buffet & clean the buffet room.
- Polishing glasses & cutlery
- Enter number of participants & docents in the lists!!! (Pre-order of a meal)
- Set up buffet for afternoon coffee break by 3 p.m.

These tasks are to be done from 15:00 to 17:00h (e.g.)

- Pay attention during coffee break, refill food and beverages, if necessary, clean up dishes as soon as possible.

- When all the event participants have left the coffee break:
- Clear coffee buffet & clean all surfaces
- Clear coffee tableware, clean tables, re-arrange chairs
- Refill drinks (stored in the cold room, wines)
- Set all tables (half board, a la carte, trainings, buses)
- Refill and clean the sugar bowls
- (If very dirty, rinse & dry well).
- Prepare the buffet room:
- Fill up crushed ice
- Get the service cutlery ready
- Fill up containers with knives and forks and place them
- Place glass bowls next to the ice chest
- Check whether there are enough small & large plates in the buffet room
- Clean the floor in the office

2.8. Checklist: Tasks of the Service Late Shift

These tasks are to be performed from 17.00 to 01.00h

- o Clarification of service arrangements (seating, drinks), meeting always at 5.30 p.m.
- o Distribute r5eserved signs, half board menus, other menu cards
- o Prepare aperitif
- o Write buffet signs, write receipts (hb)

Around 6 p.m. Set up evening buffet (see evening buffet)

- o Serve the guests
- o Clear & clean tables, change tablecloths if necessary
- o Place candles, flowers & cruets neatly again
- o Sweep chairs & benches (service- hand broom, scraper), align chairs

Approx. 20:00h clear the buffet:

- o Clean the buffet area (all surfaces, glass bonnets, ice chest, cheese cover).
- o Set up breakfast buffet (see breakfast buffet)
- o Polish glasses & Cutlery
- o In the hall: straighten tablecloths, Change them when dirty
- o If reserve tablecloths are clean, put them neatly into the cupboard, if not, to the laundry.
- o Replace burnt-out candles & tea lights: taper candles in the evening, tea lights in the morning

Cleaning the counter from 22.00h

- Empty containers
- Clean the trays, put the anti-slip pads of the trays into the dishwasher and let them dry individually.
- Clean waste bin
- Cleani the draining board & grill
- Clean the grill of the dispensing unit in the dishwasher or in the kitchen.
- Brush the taps, spray them with clear water and clean the outside.
- Clean drip tray & tiles with detergent water
- Put the grill back on
- Clean fridge doors & drawers
- Clean the counter surface area and washbasin
- Wipe and close glass cabinets
- Switch off dishwasher, let it pump empty, clean nozzles
- Clear empty bottles and full boxes
- Notes into the shift book - handover book
- Check breakfast, dinner and drinks menus for cleanliness and sort out if necessary

2.9. Checklist: End of Service - What to do?

Check all windows and lock the doors
Check/lock seminar room / meeting room
Store:
- Lock the warehouse door
- Lock the house front door
- Switch off light

Kitchen:
- Lights off in the store
- Kitchen ventilation off?

Reception/entrance
- Close door and turn off light
- Switch off copier and close window

Settlement:
- Settle bills for all tables
- Check whether all EC invoices are also settled on EC or credit card
- Tips rebooked / subtracted?
- Press Z key to conclude the day
- Copy all invoices and pack them in a plastic cover
- Check event bookings
- Put cash, cancellations (with reason and signature), EC receipts copies into an envelope and then also into the plastic cover
- Wallet remains in the safe or is taken by the head of department

2.10. Checklist: Cleaning in service

WHAT and WHEN	EARLY	LATE
Daily:		
Drinks refilled		
Drinks warehouse tidied up		
Linen cupboard		
Candles/flowers		
Cake showcase		
Buffet room clean and vacuumed		
Benches clean		
Tablecloths clean		
Trays		
Clean floor		
Polish glasses		
Cutlery polished+ refilled		
Mis-en-place		
Fold napkins		
Ashtrays, cruets, candlesticks		
Taps		
Counter drains		
Coffee maker		
Glass washer off, nozzles clean		
Ice chest		
Tidy up empties		

WEEKLY: CW _____		
Monday:		
Wine order		
Spirits order		
Dining rooms, restaurant, buffet room dusted		
Tuesday:		
Wednesday:		
Menus		
Bar menus		
Thursday:		
Wine drawer cleaned		
Candlesticks check		
Friday:		
Plate warmer		
Cruets check		
Saturday:		
Cooling basins		
Sunday:		
Glass washing machine		
Cutlery compartments		
Glass cabinets		

2.11. Circular: Breakage & Breakage List

Explanation: In order to be able to trace the breakage, each breakage is recorded in writing. The breakage list, in which every breakage is to be entered, is on the notice board /PC (WHAT was damaged? WHY was it damaged? WHO damaged it)? Breakages of large quantities or valuable items are reported immediately to the shift leader.

Breakage list:

When/date	What/pieces	Why/reason	Who/abbreviation

Taken notice   date |_____| Signature |_____|

2.12. Circular: Hygiene plan for counter

Object to be cleaned	Detergents / disinfectants	Action	Frequency
Taps	-	with brush and warm water	Daily
Sink		with hot water	Daily
Work surfaces		with hot water	Daily
Granite counter, draining boards, dispenser,		with brush, cloth, warm water	daily daily
Equipment below counter		with cloth, warm water	Asneeded , weekly
Wooden counter side surfaces		brush with hot water wash,,dry	Asneeded , weekly
Glass surfaces, glass cabinets		Warm water	As needed, Weekly
Beer glasses, beverage glasses of all kinds		Put in glasses according to work instruction	As needed
Beer/beverage pipes	is cleaned by special (company)		
Beer container closures	Hot water	Wet wipe	
Coffee maker	Milk frother; and Coffee Machine Cleaner:	Clean milk frother empty the coffee grounds, Clean hose	Daily cleaning, descaling, rinsing, etc.
Drinks fridge		Wet wipe	Asneeded , weekly
Floor	Cleaner:	Wipe, scrub wet	Daily

2.13. Circular: Restaurant service concept

Service procedure a la carte	Notes
• As soon as the restaurant opens, at least one employee must always be present in the restaurant.	
• Guests are greeted and welcomed in a friendly manner.	
• Regular guests / guests of reserved tables are addressed by name	
• Coffee, coffee specialities are offered	
• Take away excess place settings, pull trolleys into position if necessary.	
• The service is done attentively, reliably, quietly, neatly, and quickly, without disturbing the guest,	
• All food and beverages are served from the right side	
• Empty plates are cleared away. Small bowls, glasses ... are cleared with a tray.	
• Complete cutlery	
Service procedure	
• Guests are greeted and welcomed at the entrance as quickly as possible, in a friendly manner.	
• The guest is addressed by his or her name if possible	
• Serving the aperitif or the first drink within 5 minutes	
• If the guests do not want an aperitif, they are offered water.	
• Accept the drinks order	
• Assistance/recommendation with food selection	
• Acceptf the food order	
• Wine recommendation: every employee should know exactly the wines they recommend in order to be able to make a convincing recommendation	

• Set cutlery and glasses according to the menu order, then bread and dip.	
• Wine service	
• All ordered wines are to be served before the corresponding course	
• Take away the aperitif glasses as soon as they are empty	
• Starters should be served as soon as possible	
• Dishes are named when they are served!!!	
• Serving the main course, with the main component facing the guest	
• Food is served at the same time for each guest at the table, with the appropriate number of staff, in compliance with the service rules	
• Food from guests who are not present will be warmed up after asking the other guests.	
• Empty plates are cleared as quickly as possible	
• Bread, bread plates, dip are taken away , as well as cruets	
• Inquire for dessert or cheese	
• Setting the appropriate cutlery	
• After the last course, offer coffee, tea, digestif and dessert wine	
• Napkins are cleared away	

If there are children at the table, make sure that they are given a highchair if necessary. The children's menu should also be provided.

2.14. Job description: Restaurant manager

:Hotel /restaurant	Name
Department:	Restaurant management
Position name :	Restaurant Manager
Position holder:	Name of the restaurant manager
Position holder reports to:	Owner / CEO
Cooperation with:	All departments and department managers, especially with the production department/kitchen, marketing and sales, accounting and the quality officer.
Subordinate personnel	All restaurant/service staff
Position holder: represent	Colleagues
Deputy :	Colleagues / Management
Requirements profile:	Completed apprenticeship At least 5 years of professional experience Organizational skills, personnel management, English language skills
Position aim	Optimization of activities in the catering area. Monitoring of work processes in connection with the purchase of goods, storage, production and sales as well as (restaurant) guest services.
Job description/ Tasks and responsibilities	• Coordination of the entire restaurant business • Implementation of the business policy guidelines in the restaurant • Observation of competitors • Planning of the department's staff deployment, training, selection of new service employees • Planning purchasing demand, guests forecasts • Create menus, make pricing proposals in collaboration with the chef and management • Menu suggestions for special occasions in coordination with the chef and/or management • Organization of sales promotions, events, table reservations, design/decoration of the restaurant rooms • Department cost control of the

	• Organization and execution of weekly department staff meetings • Guest services: providing menu information, handling complaints, making recommendations and selling services • Preparing, , implementation and control of departmental quality standards • Checking compliance with hygiene and safety regulations in the department • Measurement of (restaurant) guest satisfaction, evaluation and introduction of suggestions for improvement • Periodic preparation of deviation reports for the top management • Carrying out other activities that are not listed here, but are ordered by top management at short notice
Work equipment:	• Hardware and (restaurant/banquet) software • Quality documentation
Working conditions:	• Depending on requirements, also irregular working hours, especially on Sundays and public holidays
Specialauthorities:	• May, in justified cases or for tactical reasons, waive payment of the bill to the guest (guest of the house) • May be granted domestic authority • Has other authoritiesas specified in the employment contract,

Taken notice: _____ date: ___ signature

2.15. Restaurant / Service Staff

Hotel / Restaurant	Name
Department:	Service
Position name:	Service employee
Position holder:	Name of the current position holder
Position holder reports to:	Restaurant manager/service manager
Cooperation with:	All colleagues in the department, the kitchen, the reception and the housekeepers' area.
Subordinated personnel	Trainees and apprentices
The position holder represents	The service manager and colleagues
Deputy:	Colleagues
Aim of the position:	Excellent service leading to maximum guest satisfaction, sale of food and beverages as well as support for conference and event participants
Job description/ Tasks and responsibilities	• Mise-en-place • Advise on the choice of food / drinks • Serving the ordered food and drinks • Keep the workplace clean / prepare it according to plan • Consider work instructions and QM documentation • Make suggestions for improvement • Carry out other activities not listed here but ordered by the management at short notice
Work equipment:	• Hardware and (restaurant/banquet) software • Quality documentation
Working conditions:	Depending on requirements, also irregular working hours, especially on Sundays and public holidays
Special authorities:	• May receive (limited) domestic authority

Taken notice / Signature   Place / Date:

2.16. Working sustainably at the restaurant

	Criteria	yes/no
1.	Purchase of bulk packs, single packs only in emergencies	
2.	Electronic water dispensers with aerators	
3.	Save energy, light with sensors	
4.	Fresh cut flowers from local / regional nurseries	
5.	Offer dishes from regional and seasonal foods	
6.	Glasswashing machine well utilised	
7.	Green electricity for the restaurant area	
8.	Green plants as air improvers	
9.	Good ventilation, if possible, no air conditioning	
10.	Instead of disinfectant, use vaporetto (steam cleaner) or hot water	
11.	No plastic dishes and plastic containers, recyclable materials instead	
12.	For guests: modern electric hand dryers, or fabric towels to be washed	
13.	Buy easily degradable cleaning agents and disinfectants	
14.	Employee training on sustainable and environmentally conscious action	
15.	Furniture made of solid wood; chairs ergonomically designed	
16.	Sort waste, organic waste to / for the compost heap	
17.	Ecological napkins; easily degradable, compostable, unbleached	
18.	Daily menus on displays, apps or recycled paper	

19.	Environmentally conscious shopping, no unnecessary packaging	
20.	Environmental management representative for all activities of the restaurant	
21.	Do without cans, plastic bottles, disposable bottles	
22.	Do not use scented stones, basin stones, scented spray, etc.	
23.	Disclaim on of paper platecloths, beer glass sleeves	
24.	WC flush with water-stop handles	

3. Quality standards for the kitchen
3.1. Work instruction: Goods receipt CCPs

CCP = Critical Control Point

Fresh Fish:

- Monitoring procedures: Visual inspection (opacity of the eyes, surface condition, consistency), odour control and/or temperature measurement (random sampling).
- Temperature: in ice or maximum +2°C (acceptance limit).
- Corrective action: Refusal to accept
- Documentation: if applicable, description of the deficiencies, record of the measured temperatures

Fresh Poultry:

- Monitoring procedures: Label control (use-by date/best-before date); visual and odour control and/or temperature measurement (random sampling).
- Temperature: see indication on the label of the packaging (maximum +4°C, acceptance limit).
- Corrective action: Refusal to accept
- Documentation: recording of the measured temperatures

Minced Meat:

- Monitoring procedures: Label control (consumption date); visual and odour control and/or temperature measurement (random sampling).
- Temperature: see indication on the label of the packaging (maximum +4°C acceptance limit).
- Corrective action: Refusal to accept
- Documentation: recording of the measured temperatures

Taken notice / Signature   Place / Date:

3.2. Work instruction: Handling fish

Delivery of fresh fish:

Fresh fish must be delivered embedded in ice or at a temperature of max. +2°C. Store fresh fish in the refrigerator / cold storage room immediately after delivery. Features for fresh fish: clear, bulging eyes with black pupils, red gills, firm fish scales, shiny surface, mucus layer must be intact, firm consistency.

Storage of fresh fish:

Store in the refrigerator/ cold storeroom in melting ice so that melting water can run off, or at max. +2°C. The fish temperature must not drop below 0°C (fresh fish must not freeze!). Store different types of fish separately. Store in clean containers with a cover to protect against contamination.

Defrosting frozen fish:

The defrosting process of frozen fish has to take place at a cooling temperature of max. +7°C in the refrigerator / cold store. When defrosting, the fish must be stored in a way that the defrost water does not come in contact with other foods and that the defrost water can drain off.

Handling fresh fish:

Only touch fresh fish with clean hands. All work on fresh fish (washing, cutting, sectioning) must be strictly separated in time from work on other raw materials.

Preparation of fish:

Complete cooking is achieved at a core temperature of 80 C for at least 3 min. or 70 C for at least 10 min. However, fish can often not be cooked completely for quality reasons.

Hand hygiene:

After touching the fresh fish, clean hands thoroughly and disinfect if necessary.

Cleaning of work utensils:

All tools such as cutting boards, knives, etc. must be thoroughly cleaned with hot water and detergent and disinfected if necessary. (Attention: Rinse off disinfectant carefully with drinking water after the required exposure time).

Taken notice / Signature: Place / Date:

3.3. Work instruction: Handling of poultry

Storing:

- Store and prepare raw poultry products and other foods separately
- Store fresh poultry meat at a maximum of +4 °C and process until the best-before date has expired.

Defrost:

- Defrosting frozen poultry meat without packaging in the refrigerator
- Dispose of packaging materials and defrost water immediately
- Clean utensils and surfaces that have come into contact with raw poultry products or defrost water thoroughly with warm water and detergent before further use.

Preparation:

- Cook poultry meat sufficiently until at least +70 °C is reached in the core of the product and the whole meat has taken on a whitish colour.

Hand hygiene:

- Clean hands thoroughly with warm water and soap between each preparation step.

Cleaning of work utensils:

- All utensils such as cutting boards, knives etc. must be thoroughly cleaned with hot water and detergent and disinfected if necessary.
- Rinse off disinfectant with water after exposure time!

Taken notice / Signature   Place / Date:

3.4 . Work instructions for cooks and kitchen assistants

Top priority: order and cleanliness at the workplace as well as clean work clothes, clean hands and arms, be healthy and ready to work;

- Comply to the cleaning and disinfection checklist as well as the checklist for kitchen activities.
- Wear work clothes and change them when dirty
- Wash and disinfect hands and forearms thoroughly before starting work, when dirty, after finishing a task and after going to the toilet.
- Do not leave cleaning and disinfecting agents containers open

Only flawless food and dishes are processed and served;

- Checking foods for perfect quality on receipt and before processing
- The dishes are prepared according to the given quality standards (recipes, instructions, photos, quantity, and quality)
- Before serving the food, check the quality: Taste, temperature, smell, quantity, colours, proportions, consistency and the visual impression.
- Switch on heat bridge and have dishes ready for lunch and later for evening business
- Deep fryer: constant control of the temperature, the quality of the fat, which is changed regularly and recorded in the checklist / kitchen book.
- Leave the ventilation running during cooking
- Salmonella risk: it is strictly forbidden to serve raw minced meat and/or desserts with raw eggs or beaten egg whites.

Optimization of goods storage and goods maintenance:

- Temperature control book: continuous control of the temperatures in the cold store, refrigerator, freezers. Recording and daily proof by signature in the book.
- Store the food separately according to the proper sorting.
  - Vegetables and potatoes
  - Potato products
  - Finished products and fish products
  - Meat and meat products
  - Ice cream
  - Pastries, bread, and rolls
- Storage in the refrigerators: separated according to assortment, in appropriate containers. Label frozen food (date, type of goods, quantity).
- Storage in cold store separately according to assortment:
  - Fish and fish products
  - Meat and meat products
  - Salads and mayonnaise
  - Cheese and cheese products
  - Fat
  - Milk and dairy products
  - Potatoes and potato products
  - Fruit and vegetable preserves
  - Fresh fruit and vegetables

Working economically:

Exact calculation and the thorough planning and preparation of the breakfast buffet, lunch, and dinner business. Is the working basis.

IN principle: no handing out of food and drinks without a voucher!!!

Taken notice   signature: Place/date:

3.5. Kitchen workflow

Workflow	Applicable work instructions
Purchasing	Production planning Purchasing specification Purchasing methods/procedures
Receipt of goods	Control procedures technical and organizational means Legal requirements
Storage	Turnover speed (first in first out) Control procedures Stocktaking Storage rules
Goods issue	Cost recording (in case of withdrawal of another department) Authorities and responsibilities Control
Preparation of kitchen works and kitchen works	Product policy Product planning Intermediate storage Equipment deployment / technical deployment Personnel deployment Standardization Quality control
Service	Restaurant Banquet Personnel deployment Service type Organization Presentation Sales promotion
Evaluation and accounting	Accounting recording Statistical recording Control procedures Key figures Short-term income statement Target/performance comparison

Taken notice   Signature: Place/date:

3.6 Food production planning:

We take the following forecasting factors into account when planning food production;

- Reservations, % of cancellations at short notice
- % of short-term bookings
- General economic situation, climate/weather
- Number of guests during the last days / trend
- Number of guests the last year/ month/ week
- Public holidays
- Different monthly utilisation / weekday utilization
- Special events in our city, region, surroundings
- External guests / passers-by
- % of guests who have lunch and/or dinner
- Effects of sales promotions and advertising campaigns

Furthermore, we rely on the sales analysis of the last few weeks or months and also calculate the degree of popularity (or at least fall back on common average values/ racers & bums list).

We calculate the popularity percentage by multiplying the number of meals sold by 100 and dividing by the total number of restaurant guests (in the same period).

Now we can predict the number of dishes:

Items according to the menu	Expected guests	Popularity in percentages	Advance calculation of the nr. of articles
Starters	120	25%	30
Main courses	120	50%	60
Desserts	120	25%	30

Purchasing specification and purchasing methods/procedures:

- Take advantage of seasonal offers
- Align item size according to least preparation loss
- Do not create a dependency relationship with the supplier, do not only buy from one supplier
- Pay attention to delivery times, avoid shopping under time pressure
- For larger quantities, pay attention to storage duration and storage space
- Include shrinkage losses, storage costs, capital formation in the calculation
- Take into account the rate of stock turnover, especially for food.
- Consider special offers
- Compare prices
- Maintain good contacts with the most important and reliable suppliers
- Also try new products
- Consider own production versus finished product purchase
- Analyze payment terms
- Consider discounts in kind
- Join purchasing co-operatives

Control tasks at goods receiving:

- Accept only ordered goods
- Check the articles to see if they meet the set standards
- Weigh, or at least spot-check, all items purchased by weight
- Randomly check all items that are delivered in boxes
- Always compare order, delivery note and invoice
- Immediately issue a meat label when accepting meat delivery if it is not present (article no., weight, price/kg, trader, date, accepted by... checked... etc.).

Proper storage:

- The necessary raw materials and supplies as well as other goods must be always available in terms of quality and quantity.

- The most common reasons that lead to food spoilage are:
- Wrong storage temperatures, too long storage times
- Lack of ventilation
- No separation of food types
- Delay between receipt of goods and proper storage

Organised goods issue:

- Goods issue only by authorized employees. Entry in goods release list
- Security precautions regarding the handover of keys, special rules possible for events
- Determination of minimum and maximum stocks per article
- Regular meat label control
- Daily control of the stock of fresh goods
- Quarterly report on the items with the lowest inventory turnover

Standardisation of quality:

- Standard purchasing guidelines
- Standardised portion sizes
- Standardised recipes
- Standardised service instructions with plate orientation, product recognition, photos
- Cook sample and co-ordinate tasting with service

Taken notice: (for all employees from the kitchen)

3.7 Checklist: Cleaning plan / Hygiene plan

OK	When	What	How and with what	Who
	After use	Tables, work surfaces, work utensils, waste bins, etc.	(hot) water, detergent, disinfectant, dishwasher, brushes, mob, bucket, cleaning cloth	Everybody
	Daily	Floor	Brushing / scrubbing, damp wiping, drying	Chef decides everybody
	Daily	Doors and walls	Cleaning, wiping	Chef decides
	Daily	Cookers, cooking pots, cooking utensils	Clean, clean, rinse	Chef decides
	Daily	Food processors	Clean with disinfectant	Chef decides
	Daily	"Garbage corner"	Clear, clean with disinfectant	Chef decides
	Monthly or more often	Window, mirror	Clean	Chef decides
	Weekly or more often	Convection oven, exhausterbonnet(s), oven	Clean with, oven cleaner	Chef decides
	Weekly or more often	Cold rooms, refrigerators, freezers	Defrost, clear, clean,	Chef decides
	Weekly or more often	Gullies, drains, channel	Eliminate blockages cleaning	Chef decides
	According to cleaning plan	Grease separator	Clean	Chef decides

See also the cleaning schedules published in the kitchen!

Taken notice: (for all kitchen staff)   Date   / Signature

3.8 Checklist: Supplier evaluation

(Main suppliers 2x per year, suppliers 1x per year)

Selection and evaluation criteria for suppliers	10/9 ☺☺		8/7 ☺		6/5 ☺		4/3 ☹		2/1 ☹☹	
Quality of the goods and/or service										
Meeting our requirements										
References										
Price, price/performance ratio										
Reliability										
Detailed product information supplied										
Support offered (technical support)										
Flexibility and interest										
Are our eventual corrective actions supported (obligation of thesupplier)										
ISO 9001 certified?										
Points achieved:										
Any complaints or claims:										

Conducted by: _____ Date: _____

3.9 Checklist for activities in the kitchen
Early shift: Breakfast

- Uniform and work protection, headgear for all employees, in the kitchen, restaurant and public areas.
- Control of the workplace (cleanliness)
- Control temperatures
- Read shift book, handover with attention to responsibilities
- Mise en place, preparation of the breakfast buffet
- Preparation of the lunch business
- Operate the lunch business
- Goods receipt and control
- Goods storage and control
- Intermediate cleaning
- Preparatory work for the late shift
- Cleaning the kitchen according to plan
- Shift handover
- Notes into Shift Book/ handover the shiftbook

Late shift: A la Carte

- Uniform and work protection, headgear for all employees, in the kitchen, restaurant and public areas.
- Goods receipt and control
- Goods storage and control
- Control of the workplace (cleanliness)
- Control of the cooling facilities and food temperatures at cooking
- Read shift book / handovers / handover book
- Preparation of the evening business / a la carte
- Operating the evening business / a la carte
- Operating of the events, according to function sheets
- Preparations for the next day or coming days
- Cleaning and disinfection of the kitchen according to plan
- Shift handover, notes into shift book

Noted: (for all kitchen staff)

3.10. Circular: Temperature controls

Month |___| Year |____|

Days	Cold store 1	Cold store 2	Cold store 3	Freezer 1	Freezer 2	Fridge 1	Fridge 2				
1.											
2.											
3.											
4.											
5.											
6.											
7.											
8.											
9.											
10.											
11.											
12.											
13.											
14.											
15.											
16.											
17.											
18.											
19.											
20.											
21.											
22.											
23.											
24.											
25.											
26.											
27.											
28.											
29.											
30.											
31.											

3.11. Circular: Food retain samples

Food Sample/ Event	Salads	Starters	Main courses	Dessert	Other food	Retain samples		Disposal of the retain samples		Signature Chef
						When	Who	When	Who	

3.12. Circular: Temperature sampling

Calendar week |_____| Year |_____|

CCP - Checklist: Temperature verification hot kitchen = 70-80° C

Control date/day	Product	Core temperature	Post-heating	Signature
(example)	Roast beef	67°C	Yes to 80° C	Mr Example
Monday				
Tuesday				
Wednesday				
Thursday				
Friday				
Saturday				
Sunday				

CCP - Checklist: Temperature control at food serving
= 65° C hot food and 07° C cold food

Control date/day	Keeping food warm	Measured temperatures	Additional heating	Signature
(example)	Soup of the day	60 °C	Short-time to 65°C	Mr. Example
Monday				
Tuesday				
Wednesday				
Thursday				
Friday				
Saturday				
Sunday				

Display of cold & hot food / buffet

- Display cold food at a maximum of 7°C, maintain temperature
- Display hot food at minimum 65°C, maintain temperature
- Limit display times to 3 to 4 hours
- Control: Permanent control of the cold & hot dishes displayed, temperature documentation (red folder)
- Attention catering: Please take samples and keep them for at least 2 weeks. Document it conscientiously

3.13. Job description: Chef de cuisine (Chef)

Hotel / Restaurant	
Department:	Kitchen
Position designation:	Chef
Position holder:	Sous chef
Position holder reports to:	Directorate
Cooperation with:	All departments, in particular with service, marketing, sales, accounting and the management's quality representative
Subordinate staff:	Kitchen staff
The position holder can represent	
Deputy:	Sous Chef
Objective of theposition :	Optimization of food production. Monitoring of work processes in connection with the purchase of goods, storage and production of food and HACCP.
Tasks and responsibilities	<ul><li>Coordination of the entire creation of dishes</li><li>Implementation of the business policy guidelines in the kitchen area</li><li>Competitor evaluation</li><li>Duty roster for 1 week in advance</li><li>Training and selection of new employees for the kitchen/production</li><li>Goods demand planning, guests' forecasts</li><li>Menu creation and suggestions for pricing, in co-operation with the management</li><li>Menu suggestions for special occasions in coordination with the management and sales department</li><li>Assistance for the organization of sales promotions and/or events</li><li>Cost control of the production of dishes</li><li>Organization, and operation of daily short meetings</li><li>Passing on relevant information to employees/ communication</li></ul>

	• Guest services: providing menu information, handling complaints, making recommendations and selling services • Preparation, introduction and control of quality standards of the kitchen catering • Checking compliance with hygiene and safety regulations in the department • Making suggestions for improvement • Periodic preparation of deviation reports for the restaurant management • Carrying out other activities not listed here but ordered by the restaurant management at short notice
Work equipment:	• Hardware and (kitchen/menu) software • Work instructions • Quality standards
Special requirements	• Training of the apprentices according to the training plan
Working conditions:	• Depending on demand, also irregular working hours, especially on Sundays and public holidays
Special authorities :	• May recommend in justified cases or for tactical reasons to waive the payment of the bill to the guest (guest of the house) • Domestic authority (MOD/Manager on Duty)

Taken notice / Signature: Place / Date:

3.14. Job description: Sous Chef

Hotel / Restaurant	
Department:	Kitchen
Position designation:	Sous chef
Position holder:	
Position holder reports to:	Chef
Cooperation with:	All departments, in particular with service, marketing and sales, accounting and the restaurant management's quality representative.
Subordinate staff:	Kitchen staff
The post holder can represent	Chef
Deputy:	Chef de partie
Objective of the position:	Optimization of food production. Monitoring of work processes in connection with the purchase of goods, storage and production of food and HACCP.
Tasks and responsibilities in cooperation with the chef	• Supporting the chef in the implementation of quality and economic goals • Coordination of the entire creation of dishes • Implementation of the business policy guidelines in the kitchen area • Competitor evaluation • Duty roster for 1 week in advance • Training and selection of new employees for the kitchen/production • Goods demand planning, guests forecasts • Menu creation and suggestions for pricing, in co-operation with the management • Menu suggestions for special occasions in consultation with the restaurant management • Assistance for the organization of sales promotions and/or events

	• Cost control of the production of dishes • Organization, and operation / participation of daily short meetings • Passing on information relevant to staff/communication • Guest services: providing menu information, handling complaints, making recommendations and selling services • Preparation, introduction and control of quality standards of the kitchen / catering • Checking compliance with hygiene and safety regulations in the department • Making suggestions for improvement • Periodic preparation of deviation reports for the management and / or plant management • Carrying out other activities that are not listed here but are ordered by the management at short notice
Work equipment:	• Hardware and (kitchen/menu) software • Work instructions • Quality standards
Special requirements	• Training of the apprentices according to the training plan
Working conditions:	• Depending on demand, also irregular working hours, especially on Sundays and public holidays
Specialauthorities:	• May recommend in justified cases or for tactical reasons to waive the payment of the bill to the guest (guest of the house)

Taken notice / Signature: Place / Date:

3.15. Job description: Chef de Partie

Hotel /restaurant:	
Department:	Catering / kitchen
Position designation:	Chef de Partie
Position holder:	
Position holder reports to:	Chef, sous chef
Co-operation with:	All departments, especially with the service,
Subordinate staff:	Trainees, apprentices, temporary staff, young chefs
The position holder can represent	Sous chef
Deputy :	
Objective of the position:	Carrying out activities in connection with the purchase department, storage and production of food, taking into account economic efficiency and in-house quality standards.
Tasks and responsibilities	<ul><li>Food preparation</li><li>Assistance with procurement planning</li><li>Guests forecasts</li><li>Assistance with menu creation</li><li>Menu suggestions for special occasions in consultation with the chef</li><li>Assistance for sales promotions and / or events</li><li>Cost control of the production of dishes</li><li>Participation in the preparation, introduction and control of quality standards of the kitchen / catering</li><li>Cleaning and checking compliance with hygiene and safety regulations in the department</li><li>Making suggestions for improvement</li></ul>

	• Carrying out other activities not listed here, but ordered by the restaurant management at short notice
Special requirements	• Supervision of trainees and apprentices
Work equipment:	• Kitchen utensils and equipment • Raw food and semi-finished or finished products • Measuring instruments (thermometers), checklists, work instructions, plans, etc.
Working conditions:	• Depending on requirements, also irregular working hours, especially on Sundays and public holidays
Special authorities:	• Has further authorities which are specified in the employment contract,

Taken notice / Signature: Place / Date:

3.16. Job description: Cook / Kitchen Professional

Hotel /restaurant	
Department:	Catering / kitchen
Position designation:	Cook, assistant cook
Position holder: Name of the jobholder	
Position holder reports to:	Chef, Sous-chef, Chef de Partie
Cooperation with:	All departments, especially with the service
Subordinate staff:	Trainees, apprentices, temporary staff
The position holder can represent:	Colleagues
Deputies:	Colleagues on an equal footing
Objective of theposition :	Carrying out activities in connection with the purchase, storage, and production of food, taking into account economic efficiency and in-house quality standards.
Tasks and responsibilities	<ul><li>Food preparation</li><li>Assistance with demand planning</li><li>Guests' forecasts,</li><li>Assistance with menu creation</li><li>Menu suggestions for special occasions in consultation with the chef</li><li>Assistance for sales promotions and / or</li><li>Events</li><li>Cost control of the production of dishes</li><li>Participation in the preparation, introduction and control of quality standards of the kitchen / catering</li><li>Cleaning and checking compliance with hygiene and safety regulations in the department</li><li>Making suggestions for improvement</li></ul>

	•	Carrying out other activities not listed here but ordered by the restaurant management at short notice
Special requirements	•	Supervision of trainees and apprentices
Work equipment:	• • •	Kitchen utensils and equipment Raw food and semi-finished or finished products Measuring instruments (thermometers), checklists, work instructions, plans, etc.
Working conditions:	•	Depending on requirements, also irregular working hours, especially on Sundays and public holidays
Special authorities:	•	Has further authorities which are specified in the employment contract,

Taken notice / Signature: Place / Date:

3.17. Job description: Steward

Hotel / Restaurant:	
Department:	Kitchen
Position designation:	Steward / scullery employee
Position holder:	
Position holder reports to:	Kitchen management
Co-operation with:	Collaboration with all kitchen and service staff as well as with the quality representative/s).
Subordinate staff:	If so interns, temporary staff new employees who are being trained
Can represent	Colleagues
Deputy	Colleagues
Aim of the position	Smooth operation in the scullery Ensuring clean (minimum) stocks of kitchen utensils, crockery, cutlery, glasses and other items
Job descriptions/ Tasks and responsibilities	• Ensure the smooth running of the stewarding area in the respective shift • Washing the crockery and cutlery • Proper operation of the dishwasher • Drying and proper storage of tableware and porcelain • Cooperation with the staff of the stewarding, service and kitchen • Cleaning of all refrigeration, storage and kitchen areas according to the kitchen's instructions and cleaning schedule. • Emptying the bins and keeping them clean • Monitoring and implementation of hygiene regulations • Cleaning the staff toilets and the lower parts of the kitchen • Other activities not listed here and ordered by the kitchen and restaurant management

Requirements for the position holder	• Possible work experience in the stewarding area / scullery area of a restaurant, hotel or large kitchen • Willingness to work alternating shifts (early, late or night shifts) and work on weekends and public holidays • German language skills an advantage • Resilience and high stress resistance • Safe handling of cleaning equipment and machines
Work equipment:	• Dishwasher(s) • Water compressor (e.g. Kärcher) • Cleaning aids (chemical and technical) • Kitchen and house cleaning quality standards
Working conditions:	• Depending on requirements, also irregular working hours, especially on Sundays and public holidays
Special authorities :	• May have authorities that are set out in the employment contract or expressed through direct instructions

Taken notice / signature:

3.18. Form: "Break List" Kitchen

This list is kept in the kitchen. Broken kitchenware, broken pots, even burnt meat dishes or spoiled goods can be entered in this list. It is an important list that helps to calculate the goods employed correctly.

When	What	How much	Who

3.19. Working sustainably in the kitchen

Environmental criteria		Yes / no, comment
1.	Separate waste according to materials	
2.	Use Aluminium foil in hot salt water instead of silver bath for the precious cutlery	
3.	Switching on ovens in the low tariff period	
4.	Use biodegradable and unbleached napkins	
5.	Steam jet cleaner for the kitchen and outdoor grill	
6.	Offer freshly prepared food	
7.	Equip deep fryers, tilt frying pans and boilers with thermostats	
8.	Gas is cheaper than electricity, therefore gas stoves in the kitchen	
9.	Sufficient space for the storage of waste	
10.	Utilize the dishwasher to full capacity (switch on when is full of dishes).	
11.	Buy bulk containers and refills	
12.	Buy green electricity from renewable sources, save energy	
13.	Connect hot water to dishwasher (saves energy)	
14.	No disposable plastic tableware / cutlery	

15. Herb garden for own consumption	
16. Kitchen and storage areas should be easy to clean	
17. Do not keep kitchen appliances on standby all the time	
18. Defrost refrigerators, during the low tariff period	
19. Refrigerators and freezers CFC-free	
20. Plastic items made from recyclable material	
21. Buy food from the region	
22. Buying food in an environmentally conscious way, without additional packaging	
23. Provable disposal of fats, oil, potato starch, etc.	
24. Avoid portion packs, portion yourself	
25. Prepare self-service buffet with open food for one hour	
26. Environmentally friendly and easily degradable cleaning agents	
27. Save water with aerators	

4. Quality Standards for Events

4.1. Workflow for the events department

Steps	Description of the workflow / Description of the activities in short form	Responsible persons Signatures
First contact Recording of guest expectations in PC software (Status: Optional or agreed. Also record customer/guest data in case of cancellations).	Every request will be answered by the event department within 24 hours by email or personal call. The customer will be made aware of our conditions in advance. In addition, a banquet folder with all the necessary information (brochures, explanations of the respective event rooms, menu and buffet suggestions, a current drink menu, general terms and conditions) is offered to the customer and sent by post or as a PDF file by e-mail. Preferably (online banquet folder). Information about the customer(s) is obtained (discreetly).	
Second contact	After 2 - 3 days, contact the customer again. Check the planned date of the event, if possible, confirm verbally in advance and give an option. Offer a viewing appointment if there is interest.	
Viewing appointment	Guided tour and presentation of the event rooms. Inquire about the wishes and the course of the event during the conversation.	
Event offer	Send the first offer to the client within 24 hours. The offer contains all necessary basic information, tips, a first (rough) cost estimate, contacts and information about our partner companies / suppliers, e.g. music, photographer, flowers, etc. Booking of the event with the respective occasions and premises. The option is maintained for 14 days. Creating an event (1 x daily folder, 1 x monthly folder)	
Planning the event	Planning takes place with the customer by telephone and in writing (email, post). This is followed by a personal consultation on site. Each planning process is answered within 2 - 4 working days upon request by the customer. Emails and phone calls are confirmed within 24 hours. On request, we offer the customer a complete package as service: planning of the event down to the last detail.	
Test dinner	This only applies to events with an estimated turnover of more than € 1,500.00. The organizer (2 persons) will be invited by us. Additional guests will	

	be charged a minimum of € 15.00 per person. At the test dinner, the chosen menu/buffet and wines will be tasted.	
Lists & Plans	The client receives seating plans and other information material (shortly) before the event.	
Service personnel briefing	Two weeks before the event, each department receives information about the event program with a schedule (function sheets, also for own events), menu, lists of names, etc.).	
Operation of the event	Is carried out using the event schedule and checklists	
Create the invoice (co-ordinate with the reservation)	4-8 weeks before the start of the event, a deposit invoice of 50% on the anticipated amount of the total invoice for our services will be sent to the client. Third-party services must be paid 100% in advance if invoiced through us. The balance will be invoiced no later than 48 hours after the end of the event.	
Event follow-up	Evaluation of guest satisfaction based on guest questionnaires (5 criteria) Analyze with the individual departments and collect ideas for improvements (suggestion scheme) Archiving of event documents and copies of invoices Inform guests about lost property left behind, if necessary Recording of customers in the guest file	
Conclusion	Prepare a function sheet / schedule. for each event	

4.2. Checklist: Workflow for events

OK / Date	Activity	Notes
	First contact: • Restaurant information • Banquet folder • Customer check	
	Second. contact: • Banquet date • Options • Viewing appointment	
	Viewing: • Site visit • Customer wishes • Banquet procedure	
	Banquet - offer (48 h): • Cost estimate with image material • Co-operation partners • Optional booking (14 days) • Create customer folder	
	Contract acceptance: • Check and countersign • Return to customer	
	Detailed banquet planning (1-4 days): • Fine-tuning with customers • Fine-tuning • A-Z Organisation	
	Test dinner: • Yes (>€ 1.500) for 2 persons • Additional guests: € 15-25/person • Coordination kitchen & service	
	Customer support: • Seating plan • Sample letters, escape routes?	
	Personnel meeting (2 weeks before): • Processes for each department • Assign of responsibilities • Interfaces / fine tuning	
	Operation of the event: • Procedure according to plan • Checklist for the reception	

	• Checklist for the service	
	Invoicing: • Down payment (4-8 weeks in advance) • Third-party services 100% in advance • Settlement after 48 h, for weddings possibly 14 days later	
	Follow-up: • Satisfaction level of the guests • Analyze with all departments and partners involved • Suggestions for improvement • Archiving the event folder • Lost property return	

Controlled by: date/time:

4.3. Checklist: Events Department Preparation & Control, 48 hours before event

OK / Time	Activity	Comment / responsibility
	Check event Information & details	
	• Check external service providers: • Music • Flowers / decoration • Wedding cake / Pastry	
	Accommodation (if hotel): • Check rooms • Lists of names • Special requests	
	• Prepare and distribute details: • Menu & Beverage cards • Place cards / table plans • Welcome letter • Gifts for guests	
	Forward short-term information & changes of the event to departments	2 weeks before (Tel.) 1 week before (Tel.)
	Check all details again (individual & standardized) on the day of the event	
Urgent work to be done:		

Controlled by   date/time:

4.4. Checklist: Tasks on the day of the event

OK / Time	Activity	Comment/ responsibility
	Checking the guest list and the wishes of the guests: Extra & children's beds, etc.	FO /Sale
	VIP arrangement, if hotel room has been booked • Plate with fruit & chocolates • a bottle of sparkling wine and water • Welcome letter from the top management • Decoration of the wedding room (Who pays?)	
	Put up signage for the event in the lobby and other premises	Remove after the event
	Flowers at the entrance on request	
	Check cleanliness in the reception area	
	Checking public spaces for cleanliness and / or forwarding according wishes to the respective department	Restaurant. / Sale
	Check flower vases (fresh flowers)	Restaurant. / Sale
	Check that newspapers and brochure holders are up to date and possibly restock them.	
	Switch on/control music (lobby & restaurant) (volume)	Restaurant. / Sale
	Update / check weather forecast	
	Check the display case with the souvenir articles for cleanliness and being up-to-date	

	Prepare wardrobe	Restaurant. / Sale
	Emptying and cleaning the outside of the ashtray	Restaurant. / Sale
	Checking the room list and guest requests	
	Distribute welcome letters & guest gifts (if desired) in the rooms	
	Check rooms (again)	Restaurant. / Sale
	Distribute menus, place cards, buffet signs, table numbers and table plan	Restaurant. / Sale
Urgent work to be done:		

Controlled by: date/time:

4.5. Checklist: Service tasks on the day of the event

OK / Time	Activity	Comment / responsibility
	Check menu box for cleanliness and up-to-datedness	
	Clean and prepare the restaurant: • Cleaning chairs, benches, and tables • Renew or order floral decoration • Cleaning cruets and candles	Cleaning Department /Restaurant/ Sales
	Chill drinks (for wine, pay attention to the vintages and colour).	Restaurant
	Control beer kegs	Restaurant
	Prepare event rooms according to the event plan: • Cleaning Tables & Chairs • Iron tablecloths and chair covers if necessary. • Set the tables according to instructions • Check glasses, cutlery, cruets, plates and candlesticks for cleanliness or polish them again. • Clean water bottles and have them ready • Prepare butter and bread plate • Service assignments by the restaurant manager	Restaurant Control: Sale

	Set-up of breakfast, cake and/or dinner buffet: • Decorate cake buffet • Set out the evening buffet with candles and decorations • For the evening and breakfast buffet, one cook and one service person are always independently responsible.	Kitchen, Restaurant
	Set-up of dessert buffet or the midnight snack will be set up on additional bar tables (where?) • always signpost dishes • and decorate	Kitchen, Restaurant
Urgent work to be done:		

Controlled by: date/time:

4.6. Job description: Event manager

Hotel / Restaurant	
Department:	Events & banquets
Position name :	Event management
Name, first name	
Position holder reports to:	Top management
Co-operation with:	All departments
Subordinate staff:	All employees of the department
The position holder can represent	The restaurant management / hotel management
Deputy:	Hotel management and / or deputy head of department
Objectives of the position: Job descriptions & tasks:	• Optimization of utilization and revenue in the event sector. • Guest services, advice, and sales • Organisation and operation of events • Agreements & correspondence with the customer • Checking all details & information against the documents • Welcoming the guests • Checking the premises and areas of responsibility of the involved departments • Short-term planning/changes at the request of the guests • Assign tasks and workplaces to external personnel, accept and control external services, if necessary • Accompanying of the event • - Farewell to the guests and satisfaction survey
Job descriptions & tasks:	• Coordination of the events & banquet department

	• Implementation of the business policy guidelines in the Events Department • Market observation • Pricing proposals • Guest correspondence • Preparation, implementation and control of departmental quality standards • Measurement of guest satisfaction, evaluation and introduction of suggestions for improvement • Carrying out other activities not listed here, but ordered by the restaurant management at short notice
Work equipment:	• Hardware and event software • Work instructions • Quality standards
Working conditions:	• Depending on requirements, also irregular working hours, e.g., Sundays and public holidays
Special authorities:	• Can design discounts to a limited extent • May be granted domestic authority • Has further authorities which are specified in the employment contract

Taken notice: date:

signature

4.7. Job description: Assistant

Hotel /restaurant:	
Department:	Events & banquets
Position name:	Event assistant
Name, first name	
Position holder reports to:	Event manager
Subordinate staff:	Trainees and apprentices
The position holder can represent:	Event manager
Deputy:	Colleagues
Objectives of the position:	Events and functions organization & planning
Job descriptions / tasks and responsibilities:	<ul><li>Conduct inquiry for partner programs</li><li>Write & modify event offers</li><li>Create statistics and lists</li><li>Carrying out other activities not listed here, but instructed by the events & banquets management or the restaurant management</li></ul>
Work equipment:	Hardware and event software
Working conditions:	Depending on requirements, also irregular working hours, e.g. Sundays and public holidays
Special authorities:	None

Taken notice:

Place/date:

4.8. Working sustainably in events and banquet department

Evaluation criteria for the event sector	10/9 ☺☺	8/7 ☺	6/5 ☺	4/3 ☹	2/1 ☹☹
Friendly natural colours					
Green electricity from renewable sources (sun, wind, water, biomass)					
Wood instead of plastic					
Information and seminar materials made of recyclable material					
Easily degradable cleaning agents and disinfectants					
Ventilation instead of air conditioning					
Sorting waste, organic waste for composting					
Regional fruit for the breaks					
Daylight					
Environmental training for event staff					
Total points:					
Suggestions:					

Six steps to success

The following six steps help to introduce the sustainable and environmental quality standards:

1. The management appoints a quality representative.
2. The quality representative communicates the quality standards part 1,2 or 3 to the heads of department, administration, reception and reservations, housekeeping, technical department, kitchen manager, service manager, etc.
3. The department heads and skilled workers adapt the quality standards assigned to them to the company-specific needs.
4. The quality representative reviews the standards and forwards them to the management.
5. After review, reconsideration and acceptance, the top management releases the quality standards.
6. Approved quality standards are mandatory for ALL employees. Each employee receives his or her standards and signs for them.

In this way, your company receives efficient and company-specific quality standards in the shortest possible time.

Good luck and confidence, your

Frank Höchsmann   Berlin, 04.07.2022

The Author Frank Höchsmann

Frank Christian Höchsmann

- Is a business economist and quality auditor according to DIN EN ISO 9000 ff.
- He can draw on many years of international experience as a quality representative, manager, and auditor.
- He worked for international companies and organisations for several years.
- During his career, he has been a trainer for more than 12,000 professionals and managers.
- Focus: Quality and sustainability management as well as international project management.

Published reference books

- Cinco pasos de la venta (Spanish)
- Efficient Marketing Concept (German, English, Spanish, Portuguese)
- Front Office (Spanish)
- Hotel Management (Spanish)
- Housekeeping (Spanish)
- Housekeeping Management (German, English, Spanish, Portuguese)
- Hygiene Management, (German, English, Spanish)
- Maître d'hotel (Spanish)
- Personnel Management for Hotels and Restaurants (German, English, Spanish)
- Quality Standards for GHotels (German, Spanish)
- Quality Standards in the Restaurant, (German, Spanish)
- Service Quality (German, English, Spanish)
- Servir con estilo (Spanish)
- Sustainable and Environmental Quality Standards for Hotels and Restaurants

Seminars, Webinars, Online Courses

Workshops for Professionals:

- o Successful Communication with the Guest
- o Housekeeping and House Cleaning
- o Hygiene Management according to HACCP
- o Sales and Additional Sales
- o Complaints and guest complaints
- o Service Quality from the Guest's Point of View

Workshops for Managers:

- o Data Protection according to EU-DSGVO
- o Efficient Marketing Concept
- o Conflict Management
- o Sustainable Quality Standards
- o Human Resources Management
- o Quality Management ISO 9001
- o Complaint Management
- o Sales Management

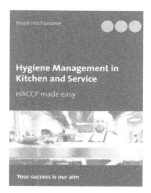

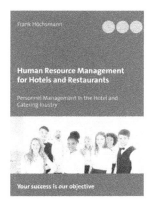

Last but not least, a request:

Dear quality interested people,
if you have any suggestions, criticism, or a proposal, you can fill in this slip and pass it on to our quality representative. Your suggestions, proposals and / or criticisms will be gratefully appreciated and registered.
If given and desired, your suggestion will be considered in the next issue.

Thank you for your cooperation.   Frank Höchsmann

My Interest Attracting Observation Written down.../ MIAOW.

_____

_____

_____

_____

Please send to Martha Cecilia Höchsmann Lozano:
m.hoechsmann@hotqua.de